# PRAYING
## in the SPIRIT

# PRAYING in the SPIRIT

## What it Really Means to Pray in the Spirit

### DENINE HAMMONDS

*Praying in the Spirit*

Copyright © 2013, 2019 by Denine Hammonds. All rights reserved.

No part of this publication may be reproduced, stored in a retrieval system or transmitted in any way by any means, electronic, mechanical, photocopy, recording or otherwise without the prior permission of the author except as provided by USA copyright law.

The opinions expressed by the author are not necessarily those of URLink Print and Media.

1603 Capitol Ave., Suite 310 Cheyenne, Wyoming USA 82001
1-888-980-6523 | admin@urlinkpublishing.com

URLink Print and Media is committed to excellence in the publishing industry.

Book design copyright © 2019 by URLink Print and Media. All rights reserved.

Published in the United States of America

ISBN 978-1-64367-937-2 (Paperback)
ISBN 978-1-64367-936-5 (Digital)

Religious

15.10.19

# DEDICATION

This book is dedicated to several people who have been a blessing to me. My husband, Frank Hammonds, who is senior pastor of Miracles Do Happen Ministries, you have supported me, stretched me, and encouraged me to go forth in ministry. I love you and appreciate your impartation in my life. You have truly been a blessing.

My daughter, Towanda Hammonds, you are very dear to me. I am honored that you are my daughter. I pray that you will continue to develop as a woman of God and a woman of prayer. Remember to always put God first in everything you do.

I would like to thank my parents, Clemon and Vernell Harris (deacon and church mother of Love Feast COGIC). Thank you for teaching me to be dedicated to the house of the Lord, to study and meditate on the word of God, and you have encouraged me to always pray about everything. I love you and appreciate you. You are truly an example of commitment to the marriage covenant. We praise God for blessing you to celebrate over sixty-six years of marriage. You are our role model and example of faithfulness and dedication.

My grandmother, Earlene Stone, "Big Mama," who is now one hundred four, you are the pillar of faith and the pillar of prayer in our family. You have blessed our entire family and so many others with your continuous prayer for salvation, holiness, healing, and a closer walk with God. You have given our family a strong spiritual heritage. Thank you for being such a blessing. Your prayers are yet being fulfilled. Thank God for answering your prayer to live to be one hundred years old. God has granted the desire of your heart.

To my husband's mom, the late Gladys Hammonds, because of her continuous prayer, her husband and all five sons received Christ and were called to preach the gospel.

# CONTENTS

Dedication ..................................................................... 5
Introduction ................................................................... 9
What is Prayer? ............................................................. 11
Types of Prayer ............................................................. 30
What Does it Really mean to Pray in the spirit? ............... 47
Praying Prophetically ..................................................... 52
Praying in other or Unknown Tongues ............................ 63
Praying for the Will of God to Be Done .......................... 73
Prayers in the Bible ....................................................... 81
Fasting and Prayer ......................................................... 90
Praying for the nations ................................................. 100
Words of exhortation ................................................... 103

# INTRODUCTION

This book sheds light on what praying in the Spirit really means. Most of the time when we use the phrase, "Pray in the Spirit," we are saying pray in tongues. Praying in the Spirit is much more than that. The key is praying a Spirit-led prayer by allowing the Holy Spirit to speak to and through your spirit. We are spirit, soul, and body. It is time for us to use and develop our spirit. We predominately only use our bodies.

It is important to pray a prayer in which the Holy Spirit puts in your spirit the utterance to speak: whether it is prophesy in prayer, praying in an unknown tongue, or praying in another tongue. The most important element is allowing the Holy Spirit to give your spirit the utterance.

Prophesy in prayer is praying in your known or native language whatever the Holy Spirit puts in your mouth and in your spirit to say. Not only are you blessed, but the whole church hears and understands the word from the Lord. Many times, the Lord will use this type of prayer to have you declare, decree, and/or command things, situations, or people to change. You can command things to come forth, set in motion, to cease, etc. God is the Ancient of Days. He knows what was, is, will be, and should be. It is crucial that we allow the Holy Spirit to use us to prophesy in prayer. The whole body of Christ is blessed with this type of prayer.

Unknown tongue is similar in that the Holy Spirit gives you the utterance, except you don't know what you are saying, because you are speaking in a language that you and no other man understands. The Holy Spirit knows and interprets what is being said. You are speaking directly to God. Your spirit is empowered when you pray in unknown tongues.

Other tongues means the Holy Spirit gives you utterance in another language. You may not know the language you are speaking, but people from another country understand what is being said. This type of praying is usually used when either you are visiting the country where that language is familiar to the people, or someone from that country is present at your service and God has a word for them. The word is more convincing to them, because it is spoken in their language. God loves us so much that he will allow things to happen such as speaking in "other tongues" to get our attention.

Trust God to allow the Holy Spirit to use you however he wants to at any time. God's will is always what is best for us personally and for the church. Let us be cognizant to be Spirit-led at all times and not just focused on what we want. God's ultimate desire is to save, to heal, to deliver, to set free, to change, to increase, to advance the kingdom, etc. When we make time to pray and listen to the voice of the Lord, we will experience another level of "praying in the Spirit."

# WHAT IS PRAYER?

Prayer, simply put, is having a conversation with God. A conversation involves both speaking and listening. We need to pour out our hearts to God. Then, we also need to listen to what God has to say about it.

Prayer involves having fellowship and sweet communion with our heavenly Father through our Lord Jesus Christ. The wonderful thing about prayer is that you can talk to God anywhere anytime. Prayer is not limited by time, place, age, language, race, denomination, or distance. Adam had the privilege of having personal face-to-face visitations from the Lord.

> And they heard the voice of the Lord God walking in the garden in the cool of the day: and Adam and his wife hid themselves from the presence of the Lord God amongst the trees of the garden.
>
> Genesis 3:8 (KJV)

> And the Lord God called unto Adam, and said unto him, Where art thou?
>
> Genesis 3:9

> And he said, I heard thy voice in the garden, and I was afraid, because I was naked; and I hid myself.
>
> Genesis 3:10

We can conclude from Genesis 3:8–10 that before this particular day, Adam was used to hearing the voice of God. He was used to being in the presence of the Lord and not being afraid. This Scripture states that the voice of God walked through the garden. This time, Adam and Eve hid themselves from the presence of God. The sin of disobedience caused Adam and Eve to be afraid of God's presence.

They had just disobeyed God and ate off the forbidden fruit. God said, "Where art thou Adam?" I believe that God is yet saying today, Adam, church, people of God, where are you? I want to fellowship with you! I want you to get in my presence! Where are you, Adam? Where are you, Eve? Where are you, church? Come before my presence. It is time for sweet communion.

Sin resulted in Adam *running from* the presence of God and being ashamed. Salvation causes us to *run to* the presence of God. Thank God that through the shed blood of Jesus Christ, we now can once again come freely and boldly before the presence of God. We can have fellowship with the Lord without fear, without doubt, and without reservation. We don't have to be ashamed of our past mistakes. We can come to God boldly, because of our present state of righteousness. Jesus died for the entire world that we might be saved.

All we have to do is receive Christ as Lord and Savior. This gives us the right, the privilege, and the authority to pray and command things to happen in the name of Jesus.

David absolutely loved to come before the presence of God. He came before the Lord with singing, playing the harp, prayer, and with thanksgiving. David even danced before the Lord and worshiped God for giving him the victory. We should likewise come before the Lord's presence with singing, worship, praise, and dancing.

> Let us therefore come boldly unto the throne of grace, that we may obtain mercy, and find grace to help in time of need.
>
> Hebrews 4:16 (KJV)

Because of Jesus, we can come boldly unto the throne of grace. We don't have to walk in fear as Adam and Eve did when they sinned. We can come with the assurance that God has great compassion for the believers. God's compassion fails not. Every day, we have been granted new mercies.

> It is of the LORD's mercies that we are not consumed, because his compassions fail not.
>
> Lamentations 3:22 (KJV)

> They are new every morning: great is thy faithfulness.
>
> Lamentations 3:23

Every morning, God has new mercies for his people! All we have to do is repent and be converted. God will forgive us of all of our inconsistencies and sins, and he will grant us new mercies daily.

Adam and Eve were thrown out of paradise because of their disobedience. Jesus became the second Adam when he died on the cross. All we have to do is repent. Then, we are forgiven. I love prayer and worship, because it can bring us right into the presence of God!

> He that dwelleth in the secret place of the most
> High shall abide under the shadow of the Almighty.
> Psalms 91:1 (KJV)

God has given us permission to come into his presence. He tells us to dwell in his presence. The presence of the Lord provides safety. It is a place of refuge. It is a covering, a shield, and a fortress for us. It is a place of deliverance. It is a place of protection. It is a place of ultimate love. Who wouldn't want to dwell in the secret place of the Most High God?

We can pray and ask God for wisdom how to enter into his presence and to teach us how to dwell, abide, and stay in his presence.

We now have the opportunity that Adam and Eve had. We have the opportunity to be in the presence of the Lord through prayer. We should make sure that we don't miss out on this great opportunity daily.

Just think, we can start right now getting in the presence of the Lord. We might as well get used to it. One day, we will eternally dwell in the presence of the Lord.

To pray literally means to hold communication with, ask, petition, beg, request, plead, supplicate, entreat, implore, or commend someone to God. Prayer is fellowship and communication between the believer and God, our eternal heavenly Father.

> And when thou prayest, thou shalt not be as the hypocrites are: for they love to pray standing in the synagogues and in the corners of the streets, that they may be seen of men. Verily I say unto you, They have their reward.
>
> But thou, when thou prayest, enter into thy closet, and when thou hast shut thy door, pray to thy Father which is in secret; and thy Father which seeth in secret shall reward thee openly.
>
> But when ye pray, use not vain repetitions, as the heathen do: for they think that they shall be heard for their much speaking.
>
> Be not ye therefore like unto them: for your Father knoweth what things ye have need of, before ye ask him.
>
> Matthew 6:5–8 (KJV)

Jesus said, "When you pray, don't be as the hypocrites."

The phrase when you pray, indicates that prayer is expected. God expects us to pray in church as a body and also one on one in private. The hypocrites only love to pray publicly so that others can view them as being spiritual. It's good to attend prayer service, prayer groups, and to pray in church, but that does not negate our individual time alone with God.

God desires us to spend time alone with him in prayer. When we pray, we are coming before the throne of God. This is considered our "closet" or the "secret" place. No one should be allowed in our alone time with God, because this is our special time to talk to God and for God to reveal himself to us.

Jesus tells us not to use vain repetition in prayer. Vain can mean having no real value, proud, arrogant, haughty, egotistic, useless, worthless, hopeless, and unprofitable. Repetition means boring, wordy, or continually repeating the same thing over and over.

Jesus was teaching the disciples to pray with meaning and purpose. Jesus doesn't want us to come before the presence of God heady, high minded, full of pride, as if we are in control and can control God. God is Lord of all! He is all knowing, all seeing, the only wise God, Alpha, Omega, the Beginning and the End, the First and the Last, Jehovah, the Ancient of Days, the Creator of everything.

We should enter prayer with tremendous reverence for God, in the fear of the Lord. We should pray, having faith in the word of the Lord and with total trust that God is able to do exceeding and abundantly above anything our minds can imagine.

Praying hopeless, doubting, and faithless prayers is futile. We waste so much time coming before the Lord complaining, throwing temper tantrums, whining about the same things for years. God is the problem solver. He already knows what we need. He will hear and answer our prayers when we come in agreement with the word of God, expecting and trusting him to deliver.

Jesus taught his disciples the model type of prayer to pray in Matthews. Many of us have quoted it for years without understanding its full meaning.

> After this manner therefore pray ye: Our Father which art in heaven, Hallowed be thy name.
>
> Thy kingdom come. Thy will be done in earth, as it is in heaven.
>
> Give us this day our daily bread.
>
> And forgive us our debts, as we forgive our debtors.
>
> And lead us not into temptation, but deliver us from evil: For thine is the kingdom, and the power, and the glory, forever. Amen.

For if ye forgive men their trespasses, your heavenly Father will also forgive you:

But if ye forgive not men their trespasses, neither will your Father forgive your trespasses.
Matthew 6:9–15 (KJV)

*Our Father who art in heaven* indicates a relationship with God. It verifies that we are the children of God. This qualifies us to be heirs, children of the King of Kings. It also gives us access to God boldly in prayer. As a result of the death of Jesus, we know God like no previous generation. We know God as Abba Father meaning "Daddy God." Our relationship with God should be closer than any other relationship.

*Hallowed be thy name.* Holy, awe, sacred is thy name. We should always enter prayer with reverence for the name of our God, the Great I Am that I Am. We should realize that God has the solution to any dilemma we may have. All answers come from God. He is all knowing and all seeing. Therefore, we acknowledge through faith in Jesus that whatever we need, desire, or seek, God is able to perform it.

It is a privilege to be able to enter directly into the holy of holies without having to go through the priest. We don't have to be afraid or ashamed. We can come before the greatest King of all times, knowing God is our daddy, and that it pleases him to bless us and bring us into his purpose for our lives.

*Thy kingdom come* refers to Christ's full reign on the earth. There will come a time when Jesus himself shall sit upon the throne of David who was considered the greatest king of all times. Jesus the Messiah shall rule and reign and sit upon the throne of David forever and ever. Jesus is currently reigning through the saints today. Jesus told the parable in Luke 19:13 to "occupy until I come." *Occupy* simply means to take possession of, control, take over, or command. The saints are supposed to have an effect in the earth. We are not to be like the world, but we are to be the answer for the world. The church is supposed to be the lender and not the borrower, above and not on the bottom. We are supposed to be standing and reigning in the place of Jesus. We are supposed to be walking in authority, binding and loosing.

The most effective way that we can rule in the earth is through prayer. We are supposed to be operating in kingdom principles not in worldly principles.

Lord, help us to conform to your will! Lord not the will of our flesh or the will of the enemy, but let your will be done in the earth through the saints! God ultimately knows what is best. After all, God is the beginning and the end, the first and the last, the Ancient of Days. He is the only wise God and creator of everything.

Jesus said, *"Give us this day our daily bread."* It is not a sin to pray for provision if that is what you need. We can be confident that God desires to meet our every need and grant every desire of the heart according to his will. However, as we grow in God, we will see a shift in our status. We will move from having to ask for provision to being providers to others. God wants the church to be in a place of authority. We are no longer in bondage to sin. We are free from sin, free from poverty, free from the curse of the law, free from the curse of our forefathers. We are adopted sons and daughters of the King of Kings. Our mind-sets need to change. We need to start walking and being kingly descendants, royalty, and spiritual-minded people.

*Forgive us our debts, as we forgive our debtors.* If someone owes you something and never pays it back, forgive them anyway. God forgave us of all of our sins. We will never be able to pay God for the redemption of sin. Yet Jesus shed his blood, and we are free from sin. We owe no debt. It was paid in full at Calvary. As Jesus forgave us, so are we to forgive others. Your forgiveness of others frees you to be forgiven.

*But if ye forgive not men their trespasses, neither will your Father forgive your trespasses.* First of all, unforgiveness will keep you from the presence of God. Also, if you refuse to forgive others, God will refuse to forgive you. God will not listen to or answer your prayers if you are holding grudges. God expects us to deal with our issues. Go to the person who did you wrong. You can tell the person that they hurt you, but that you forgive them. Then let it go! If they apologize, accept their apology. If they don't apologize, you must forgive them anyway. God only holds us accountable for what we do. If you refuse to forgive, you are causing harm to your own self and holding in bondage the person you should forgive. Forgive and let go! It will free you to receive what God has in store for you. Thank God for the spirit of forgiveness. It is not always easy to forgive, but by the grace, mercy, and love of God within us, we can forgive.

## PRAYING IN THE SPIRIT

Prayer includes praise, worship, thanksgiving, adoration, supplication, confession, and petitions to the Lord Jesus Christ.

> Be careful for nothing; but in everything by prayer and supplication with thanksgiving let your requests be made known unto God.
> Philippians 4:6 (KJV)

> And the peace of God, which passeth all understanding, shall keep your hearts and minds through Christ Jesus.
> Philippians 4:7

This Scripture tells us not to worry or become distressed about anything, but in everything, communicate our concerns, needs, desires, and request to our heavenly Father. Then, we are to believe that he will answer prayer.

God wants us to bring our troubles, worries, and fears to him and allow him to deal with the frustrating situations and trials of life. Think about it: the Lord already knows everything we need before we ask him. He is an all-knowing God. So we should pray to God in honesty and in faith, based on the written word of God (the Bible). God will answer prayer.

> And He spake a parable unto them to this end, that men ought always to pray and not to faint.
> Luke 18:1 (KJV)

Jesus was very serious about prayer. It was Jesus who said that we should "always pray" and not faint in prayer. When we faint, we become weary, weak, feel hopeless, depressed, and lose courage. We must be strong in the Lord and not become weary in the battles of life or weary in prayer.

It is important to pray daily throughout the day. Prayer is a necessity for every Christian. Think about it. There are very few things that you always do. You don't always eat. You don't always sleep. You don't always work. You don't always travel. You don't always go to church, but Jesus said, we should "always pray" and not faint.

We should not wait until the problems in life are so heavy that we don't know what to do. We should pray when we are happy. Pray when we are upset. Pray when things seem to be in order. Pray when things are out of order. Prayer should be part of our normal daily schedule. When we wake up in the morning, we can pray and thank God for grace, mercy, love, favor, provision, and peace. Throughout our day, we can pray for God's direction, favor, guidance, forgiveness, forbearance, and patience with others. We should pray that God's will be done in our lives and in the church. We should pray for our leaders, family, friends, neighbors, country, and the world. Before we go to sleep at night, we should pray and thank God for all blessings throughout the day. We can pray that God will give us a peaceful sleep.

> Pray without ceasing.
>
> 1Thessalonians 5:17 (KJV)

# PRAYING IN THE SPIRIT

Pray in your mind and in your heart all throughout the day. The devil never ceases to kill, steal, and destroy. So we should never cease to pray. We should also keep our ears open to hear what God is saying. That is also part of our prayer experience.

> Confess your faults one to another, and pray one for another, that ye may be healed. The *effectual fervent prayer of a righteous man availeth much.*
> James 5:16 (KJV)

Our prayers should be effectual, meaning our prayers should be able to produce the desired outcome. We should not waste our prayer time complaining, crying, and talking about what we wish we had or what we didn't get.

An effectual prayer is a prayer of faith. You can have an effectual prayer by finding Scriptures in the Bible consistent with your prayer request. Simply use the Scripture to pray the prayer of faith.

Father, I need healing. Your word says in 1 Peter 2:24, *"By whose stripes ye were healed."* So I apply your word to my body. My healing took place when Jesus died on the cross. He died for my salvation, healing, and deliverance. Therefore, I decree and I declare that according to the word of God, I am healed. I was healed, and I will be healed. Lord, I thank you for my healing in the name of Jesus!

This is an example of praying a valid prayer, a prayer that produces the desired results.

Around ten years ago, I was diagnosed with Graves Disease, which is a type of hyperthyroidism. The hyperthyroidism caused my heart to accelerate at such a fast pace that my doctor said she was amazed that I had not experienced a heart attack. I was under the care of a cardiologist, internal medicine, ENT, and gynecologist. I was hospitalized a few times for about a week each time. I had weekly blood test appointments to monitor my thyroid. After about a year, my thyroid went from hyper to hypothyroidism. One particular day, I had vomited continuously and was extremely sick. I remember praying and saying, "Lord I believe your Word that says by the stripes of Jesus I am healed. I know that you are a healer. Lord, I need to hear from you. I don't understand why I am sick. If it is not my time to die, then heal me. If it is my time, then I am ready." The Holy Spirit spoke to me and said, "You shall live and not die. You have an assignment to complete."

Day by day, little by little, I began to recover. I continued to pray and confess that I am healed. Almost every day during this process I felt led to listen to a song, "It's Only a Test" by Bishop Larry Trotter from Chicago. One day as my husband was driving me to the hospital, he told me that he had heard this song on one of our CDs. He said, "I believe this song is for you." He played "It's Only a Test!" I believe that was a confirmation from the Lord that the sickness that I was going through was only a test. That was such a great encouragement.

After around two years, I went to the cardiologist for a checkup, and he completely released me. He said, "Your heart is in excellent condition. Only, I have no records of when I did your surgery." I said to him, "You never did surgery for my heart." He expressed emphatically that it was impossible for my heart to have returned to the excellent condition that it was in without having done surgery. He articulated that he had seen the condition of my heart, and it was medically impossible for my heart to reverse from the condition it was in, back to being in an excellent condition. With God all things are possible! God healed and restored my heart.

Next, I went to my appointment with my doctor, who specialized in internal medicine. He also gave me a release. He said, "I can say this now. We thought you were a goner. We did not expect you to live. You were in such bad health." He said that I didn't have to come back to have blood drawn weekly anymore. I should follow up in a year for an annual checkup. Praise God for answered prayer of healing. This was not an experience that I would have desired to go through, but I learned so much about the process of healing and walking by faith for healing through this experience. It has helped me to be more compassionate with those who are sick and believing God for their healing. I also learned that my purpose is keeping me alive!

You must pray according to the word of God in the name of Jesus. The word of God is the will of God. Be sure to pray according to the word of God in order for your prayer to be effective.

> And this is the confidence that we have in Him that if we ask anything according to His will He

heareth us, and if we know He hears us, *whatsoever we ask we know* that we have the petitions that we desire of Him.

1 John 5:14 (KJV)

We should ask in faith and not waiver. John says that God will hear us if we pray according to the will of God. If our prayer is heard, it will be answered. God does not hear prayer without answering prayer. To say that God hears our prayer means God is giving audience to our prayer. He is paying attention. He is listening, and God will answer in time and on time.

God does not hear our prayer when we pray out of the will of God. When we pray outside of God's word, we are praying an invalid prayer. God does not give audience to an invalid prayer. Therefore, God does not answer invalid prayers. It is a prayer that produces nothing.

> He that turneth away his ear from hearing the law, even his prayer shall be abomination.
>
> Proverbs 28:9 (KJV)

If we refuse the law of God, God will not answer our prayer. God's word is the law and will of God.

James also mentioned that we should pray a fervent prayer in James 5:16. A fervent prayer is passionate, earnest, hot, serious, and intense.

Remember in Luke 22:44 when Jesus prayed in the garden of Gethsemane?

# PRAYING IN THE SPIRIT

> And being in an agony He prayed more earnestly: and his sweat was as it were great drops of blood falling down to the ground.
>
> Luke 22:44 (KJV)

This Scripture describes the events that took place right before Jesus was crucified. He went to the garden to pray. He took the twelve disciples with him. They fell asleep while he prayed. Jesus knew that the hour of his crucifixion was imminent. He was well aware of the great persecution and pain that he was about to experience. Some believe that a blood vessel burst in his head as he prayed, causing blood to gush out of his head. We do know that Jesus prayed an extremely intense prayer. Then, Jesus prayed even more earnestly until his sweat was as it were great drops of blood falling down to the ground. Talk about fervent prayer! It doesn't get more fervent than that!

We need to follow our example, Jesus, who set aside some time to pray in a secret place. We should go to a quiet place where we can pray without disturbances. There are times when we have good intentions to pray. Then, it seems like we have all kinds of interruptions. The telephone rings. It's someone you haven't heard from in a long time. The doorbell rings. It is someone you have not seen in years. The baby starts to cry. Distractions, distractions, distractions, all kinds of distractions come about to hinder us from our time with God in prayer. I have even fallen to sleep while praying. So did the disciples.

Jesus got up a great while before day. While others were asleep, Jesus used that early morning time to pray. We really need that quiet time to be alone with the Lord to pour out our hearts to him and to listen to our Father. There is something special about early morning prayer. We can avoid so many disruptions. It's peaceful, quiet, the rising of a new day. It seems to be the perfect time for prayer, worship, and a time of letting go of yesterday and moving forward toward the new beginning.

Our prayer time should also include worship and thanksgiving, not just asking the Lord for things. Worship is one of the best ways to begin prayer. Give God adoration! Magnify the name of the Lord! Give God glory and honor! Worship the beauty of His holiness!

> Let us come before His presence with thanksgiving,
> and make a joyful noise unto Him with psalms.
> Psalms 95:2 (KJV)

We can enter the presence of the Lord with thanksgiving and making a joyful noise. We can enter with singing, and praising, and worshiping.

Many times, people think that they will run out of things to pray for. There are so many things that we need to pray for. I believe that is the reason Jesus instructed us to always pray and not to faint. Below is a list of just a few of the things we need to pray for on a regular basis:

- Healing
- Deliverance
- Guidance/direction
- Our family
- Our local church and the whole body of Christ
- Oneness in the body of Christ
- Our spiritual leaders (apostles, prophets, bishops, pastors, teachers, missionaries, and evangelist)
- The purpose of God be accomplished
- Wisdom, understanding, knowledge, counsel, and might
- That we become doers of the word and not hearers only
- That the gospel would be preached in every nation and to every kindred of people
- Others (intercession)
- Leaders of the land (political leaders, the president, kings, mayors, governors, supervisors, etc.)
- Peace in Israel
- People on our job
- Neighbors

The list goes on and on. The key is to pray in faith continuously, consistently, and according to the word of God.

# TYPES OF PRAYER

Let's take a look at the various types of prayer.

- Prayer of faith
- Prayer of intercession
- Prayer of thanksgiving
- Prayer of Petition/request

## THE PRAYER OF FAITH

Every prayer should be prayed in faith. When you pray, you must believe that God can and will accomplish the thing that you pray for.

> And the prayer of faith shall save the sick, and the Lord shall raise him up; and if he have committed sins, they shall be forgiven him.
> 
> James 5:15 (KJV)

> Confess your faults one to another, and pray one for another, that ye may be healed. The effectual fervent prayer of a righteous man availeth much.
> 
> James 5:16

# PRAYING IN THE SPIRIT

> Elias was a man subject to like passions as we are, and he prayed earnestly that it might not rain: and it rained not on the earth by the space of three years and six months.
>
> James 5:17

> And he prayed again, and the heaven gave rain, and the earth brought forth her fruit.
>
> James 5:18

James says the prayer of faith will save the sick and the Lord will raise him up. The prayer of faith is able to bring salvation, healing, and deliverance. Sometimes, people feel like they are too discouraged or weak to pray. We can pray for them or with them in the name of Jesus and God will honor our prayer.

> And Elijah the Tishbite, who was of the inhabitants of Gilead, said unto Ahab, As the Lord God of Israel liveth, before whom I stand, there shall not be dew nor rain these years, but according to my word.
>
> 1 Kings 17:1 (KJV)

Elijah prayed that there would be no rain in Gilead according to his word. The Lord listened to and answered the prayer of Elijah. Immediately, God charged Elijah to leave town and go near Jordan by the brook of Cherith, where he had access to plenty of water. Eventually there was a drought in the land and the brook dried up because there had been no rain. When his assignment was up at Cherith, God told Elijah to get up and go to Zarephath, where a widow would make provision for him. God always looks out for his people. Even in the midst of an economic crisis, God always makes provision for his children.

And Elijah said unto Ahab, Get thee up, eat and drink; for there is a sound of abundance of rain.

So Ahab went up to eat and to drink. And Elijah went up to the top of Carmel; and he cast himself down upon the earth, and put his face between his knees,

And said to his servant, Go up now, look toward the sea. And he went up, and looked, and said, There is nothing. And he said, Go again seven times.

And it came to pass at the seventh time, that he said, Behold, there ariseth a little cloud out of the sea, like a man's hand. And he said, Go up, say unto Ahab, Prepare thy chariot, and get thee down, that the rain stop thee not.

1 Kings 18:41–44 (kjv)

Prayer includes making a command in the name of Jesus. Elijah commanded the elements that it would not rain. He declared that there should not be any dew or rain. There was no rain on the earth for over three years.

After the season of drought, Elijah prayed again that it would rain. God answered his prayer by first shutting up the rain. Then when the prophet prayed again after three years and asked for the rain to come, God granted the request of the prophet and sent the rain. Elijah prayed over the elements in faith, and God brought it to pass.

Jesus likewise rebuked the winds and the storm and said, "Peace, be still." The storm ceased at his command. God has given us authority to pray even over the wind, sea, rain, trees, people, land, earth, etc! Prayer is powerful in the name of Jesus!

In Luke 7:2–7, the centurion's servant was dying. The centurion felt unworthy that Jesus should come to his house. He requested that Jesus simply send his word of command to heal his servant. He recognized that because Jesus was in authority that his words carried authority. He realized that Jesus did not have to necessarily come and lay hands on the servant. All Jesus needed to do was send the command, and it would be done. The centurion being in authority understood authority. He had faith that his servant would be healed at the word or command of Jesus. Jesus did indeed send his word of healing, and the servant was healed in that same hour. The prayer of faith and the prayer of intercession healed this servant. We have been given access to use the name of Jesus even to use the prayer of faith to call those things that are not as though they were. Jesus did not lay hands on the servant or even see the servant. This proves that the person does not have to be present for prayer to work. Prayer has no boundaries or limitations. Doubt and unbelief are the only hindrances to prayer. Prayer can be a form of a command in the name of Jesus!

Remember, every prayer should be prayed in faith. Find Scriptures in the Bible that are in agreement with what you are praying for. Believe God for what you are asking. You may not see it in the natural immediately, but believe God for the answer and ignore what you see in the natural. Pray the desired result. Believe that God can and will accomplish that which you pray.

## PRAYER OF INTERCESSION

The prayer of intercession is petitioning God on behalf of someone else. There are times when we pray for our families, friends, people we know, and people we have never met in person.

In Acts 9:38–40, Tabitha died. The people came to Peter and told him that he had to do something for this woman. She had used her talent and made clothes for the poor. Peter prayed for Tabitha and then commanded her to wake up from the dead.

Prayer is not restricted by circumstance, situations, or status quo. You can pray for people, places, things, or elements. You can pray for other countries and nations. God will honor your prayer of faith and intercession. Prayer is not hindered by distance or obstacles! It is only hindered by doubt, disobedience, and unbelief.

When I was pregnant with my daughter, I experienced morning sickness twenty-four hours a day, seven days per week. By the time I was three months pregnant, I had become very dehydrated. I was losing weight so fast that my physician put me in the hospital. My grandmother, whom we call Big Mama, also affectionately known as Mother Stone, called me from Flint, Michigan, and prayed for me over the telephone. She prayed that I would be healed. She prayed that I would not lose the baby. She also prayed that I would have an easy delivery.

It was not until after I had delivered my daughter that I fully understood the impact of her prayer. When it was time for me to deliver the baby, I remember the doctors coming and going in the delivery room, whispering to each other and looking at me weirdly. My doctor kept asking me if I was okay. I kept saying I'm fine. At first, I thought it was normal procedure. Then, they kept whispering and asking if I was sure that I was okay. I expressed to my doctor that I wanted to get up and walk around because I was tired of lying on my back. Other doctors and technical people kept coming in and out my room. I became very suspicious. I asked my doctor what was wrong. At first, she said nothing. The doctors kept coming and going and whispering and looking strange. So I asked again if they would please tell me what was going on. My doctor pulled off some of the sheets to the monitor that I was hooked up to and said, "This machine monitors your pain. Do you feel anything?" My response again was no. She asked,

"What exactly are you experiencing?" I told her that I just felt a little discomfort from lying down and wanted to get up and go walking. She responded that according to the monitor, the pain level that I should have been feeling indicated the pain was off the chart. In other words, the machine was showing my pain was immeasurable for the past few hours. They could not believe that I was holding a conversation with them and not yelling, screaming, throwing things, etc. She had the machine checked to make sure it was working properly. Then, they even switched the machine with other patients that were yelling and screaming due to their pain level. She had asked the other doctors to come to witness what was happening. Everyone agreed that this was the first time that they had seen a pregnant woman, about to deliver, experiencing pain at such a high level holding a calm conversation. They could not believe that I did not feel the tremendous pain. My doctor was an experienced ob-gynecologist. The other doctors were specialists as well. They expressed that this was highly unusual, and they would not have believed it, if they had not seen it for themselves.

Weeks later, I went to my doctor for a checkup. She reiterated to me how amazed she was that I did not feel the pain. I had a normal delivery. Everything went fine. I was blessed with a healthy baby girl. Talk about an answer to prayer.

Months later, I recalled that my grandmother had prayed for me over the telephone that I would have an easy delivery. I believe that God granted her request. Talk about the power of intercession. Her prayer had been for my imminent healing and for my future delivery of the baby. Both prayers were answered.

Thank God for Big Mama's prayers. God does answer prayer. God is yet working miracles every day.

> I exhort therefore, that, first of all, supplications, prayers, intercessions, and giving of thanks, be made for all men;
>
> For kings, and for all that are in authority; that we may lead a quiet and peaceable life in all godliness and honesty.
>
> 1 Timothy 2:1–2 (KJV)

Timothy tells us to pray for all of our leaders. We should pray for our natural leaders and our spiritual leaders: apostles, prophets, evangelists, pastors, ministers, elders, missionaries, teachers, mothers, ministers of music, administrators, helps, and governments. Our leaders need our faithful prayers and support. There are those who waste time tearing down our leaders. They don't need gossip, backbiting, disrespect, and rebellion. Our leaders need much prayer.

We can pray that our spiritual leaders would be faithful, holy, wise, obedient to God, focused on souls, and examples of the believer. Pronounce blessing over their families, finances, and ministries.

We should pray that the body of Christ would grow and mature in Christ. We come to Christ as a baby, but we are not to remain Christian babies all of our lives. We are to mature and grow in God and grow in grace. The church should be a house of worship, a house of prayer, and a training center for the saints. All saints have the ministry of reconciliation. When God saves us, it should become our mission to minister to others and bring others to Christ. When was the last time you won a soul to Christ? Begin to pray and ask the Lord to help you win souls to the kingdom of God. It's all about the kingdom of God!

We should intercede for others. Jesus prayed for the disciples that their faith would fail not. We should pray that others will be healed, delivered, saved, and set free. Pray for this generation to turn to Christ. Pray for our young people. There are so many hurting, confused, addicted, and traumatized young people. They need our constant prayers, love, and support.

We should pray that the gospel of Jesus Christ would be preached in all the nations of the earth. Support those that are spreading the gospel to other nations through prayer and financial support.

The Scripture tells us to pray for the peace of Jerusalem. Israel is God's chosen. We as Christians have been engrafted in. However, God still loves his firstborn Israel and wants us to pray for them and bless them. God will bless those that bless Israel.

We must pray for our natural leaders (the president, mayors, and governors, etc.). We should pray for our supervisors on our job. We should pray that all of our leaders make wise and godly decisions. It doesn't matter what political party they represent or if we voted for them or not.

It is still our obligation as a Christian to pray for our leaders that their decisions would bring peace instead of confusion. Pray that their decisions will be a blessing in the earth and for the saints.

The saints prayed for Peter to be released from prison. It happened so fast that they didn't believe Rhoda when she told them Peter was at the door. An angel of the Lord arrived on the scene and released Peter from prison as a result of an effective prayer. Prayer is the key that unlocks the door.

## **PRAYER OF THANKSGIVING**

> Be careful for nothing; but in everything by prayer and supplication with thanksgiving let your requests be made known unto God.
>
> Philippians 4:6 (KJV)

> I will praise the name of God with a song, and will magnify him with thanksgiving.
>
> Psalms 69:30 (KJV)

It is a good idea to worship God even before you make your request known. God already knows your request before you ask anyway. He desires us to come before his presence with singing, thanksgiving, worship, trust, faith and hope. Even as we are making our request known, we should not forget to give God the glory that is due unto his holy name. As we worship and thank God, it will remind us of his awesomeness and ability to do exceedingly, abundantly above all that we could ask or think.

Sometimes, our situation seems so overwhelming. When we remember how great, awesome, and powerful God is, our problem will suddenly seem insignificant and small.

Many times as we worship in prayer, the answer to the request comes to our mind. God just plants it in our spirit and mind. Discernment and understanding comes; knowledge and revelation is brought to light in our situation. God loves for us to come before his presence with thanksgiving and worship.

## PRAYER OF PETITION

When we ask God to do something, change a situation, bless our finances, or protect our family, we are praying the prayer of petition. In this type of prayer, you simply make your request known unto God. Even though the Lord already knows what we need before we ask, God still tells us to ask in faith, nothing wavering, make our request known unto God.

Parents are the same way with their children. Sometimes, we wait for our children to ask, and at other times, we have already done it before they ask. God is our heavenly Father, and God gives good gifts to his children.

> If a son shall ask bread of any of you that is a father, will he give him a stone? or if he ask a fish, will he for a fish give him a serpent?
> 
> Luke 11:11 (KJV)

# PRAYING IN THE SPIRIT

A good father will not give his son a serpent if his son asks for fish. God will not give us a stone if we ask for bread. God is a just, fair, and loving God! So we can come to God in prayer, with thanksgiving making our request known unto him.

I remember at the age of thirty I had developed a lump under my arm. My family physician recommended that I have a biopsy to test for cancer. I agreed to have the biopsy, but I was praying and believing God to be cancer free. After the results came back, the doctor informed me that I had breast cancer and that he recommended I have a mastectomy. I told him that I was not going to have a mastectomy, and that I did not believe I had cancer. He expressed that he would send my results to another specialist. They said the same thing. He sent it to two specialists, who concurred. I kept saying, "No I don't have cancer." Finally, he sent it to the Mayo Clinic. He contacted me and said he didn't know what happened. The Mayo Clinic agreed that my cells were odd, but there was no sign of cancer. The prayer of faith does work. That was twenty-two years ago. God is faithful! God is a healer! By the stripes of Jesus Christ I am healed.

- King Jehoshaphat and the children of Israel prayed concerning a battle. God gave the people what to do. God also fought the battle for them. "The Lord shall fight for you and ye shall hold your peace." God is Jehovah-Nissi, the Lord our banner. He always goes before us, causes us to triumph, and gives us the victory.

- Jesus taught the disciples to pray, "Give us this day our daily bread." When taxes needed to be paid, Jesus told Peter to go and get money out of the mouth of the first fish. It was enough to pay taxes for both of them. God is Jehovah-Jireh, the Lord whose provision shall be seen, experienced, and manifested.

- Hezekiah prayed the prayer of petition for God to extend his life. God answered his prayer and added years to his life. God is the creator and life giver. He is Jehovah-Elohim, which means preserver, creator, mighty, and strong.

- Hannah prayed for a male child. God healed and opened up her barren womb and gave her the great prophet Samuel and other children. God is a God of multiplication. God is Jehovah-Rophe, the Lord who heals spiritually, emotionally, and physically.

- Jacob (Israel) prayed over all of his children before he died. He prophesied to each of them. He was truthful with all of his children about their good and bad qualities. He also prayed for his grandchildren through the seed of Joseph. Jacob crossed his hands to put his right hand on Ephraim and his left hand on Manasseh. He pronounced the special blessing on Ephraim who was the younger of the two sons. This was not the traditional way to bless the seed. The older usually received the greater blessings. Sometimes when we obey God, it goes against our traditions. When Jacob crossed his hand to bless Ephraim, Joseph attempted to switch Jacob's hand to make sure that the older received the greater blessing. Jacob let Joseph know that he knew what he was doing. He was choosing God's way instead of tradition. He learned through his own life experience that God's way is not always the way it's always done. God way is always the best way. We must learn to hear God in every situation. God gives wisdom to saved parents. God is all knowing and all seeing. God is the Ancient of Days.

- The thief on the cross made the request of Jesus, "Lord, remember me when you come into your kingdom." Jesus said, "This day, you shall be with me in Paradise." God granted his request. God is Jehovah M'Kaddesh, the Lord who sanctifies, the Lord who makes whole.

- Daniel faced the Holy City, Jerusalem, and prayed three times per day. He was thrown in a den of lions for praying to the God of Abraham, Isaac, and Jacob. Daniel used the lions as a pillow when he fell asleep in the den of hungry lions. God's protection will not only save your life, but God will use adversity to bring you comfort in the midst of your trial. God is Jehovah-Shammah. He is always with us, even in times of trouble.

- Jesus prayed and blessed the two little fish and five loaves of bread. The little boy's lunch multiplied. His lunch fed 5,000 men, not including the women and the children. Plus, they had food left over. Think about it. Usually, there are three times as many women as there are men in a crowd. Not to mention all the children that would have been there. There could have easily been over 20,000 people there. When you provide the seed, God will meet your need. God will not only bless you, but he will make you a blessing to others. He is El Shaddai. The All-Sufficient One.

- Peter and the disciples prayed for boldness to preach and minister the gospel of Jesus Christ. Some messages require boldness to speak, especially when it is a word of correction. People, as a whole, want to be encouraged and flattered. Many people have a hard time receiving correction and warning. A wise man receives correction and a word of change, but a fool rebels and continues in his foolishness.

- Anna prayed in the temple daily. She saw the Messiah Jesus before her death. That had been one of her prayers. She wanted to see the Messiah before her death. God will answer prayer, reveal things to you and show you things that are to come.

- Samson prayed that the Lord would avenge him of his adversaries. Samson's enemies had put out his eyes, but God restored his supernatural strength. Samson killed more people at his death than in his lifetime. God will strengthen you and cause you to accomplish great and mighty things. Things you didn't even know that you were capable of doing. With God, all things are possible to him that believeth.

- Paul and Silas praised and prayed at midnight. The prison shook like an earthquake and set them free. God pours out his anointing on his people to destroy every yoke and bondage of the enemy.

- Moses prayed at the Red Sea. God opened up the Red Sea and congealed the waters. The waters became a wall for the children of Israel, but drowned Pharaoh and his army. Who is like unto the Lord, our God?

- Jabez prayed that God would bless him indeed meaning without a doubt. He also prayed that God would enlarge his territory. He also prayed that he would not cause harm to others as his name indicated. God will change your name to a good name and prosper you despite your past. Just as God changed Abram to Abraham, which means the father of many nations, God caused him to prosper above all nations. God gave Abraham innumerable seed.

- Jesus prayed in the garden of Gethsemane. "Father, not my will, but thy will be done." God expects total commitment. He expects us to live our life to please him. We have to constantly remind ourselves that it is not about us, but it is all about Jesus and the purpose and destiny of God for our lives. It is about impacting the kingdom of God.

- Queen Esther prayed for her nation. The children of Israel fasted and prayed with her. Then, she risked her life and went before the king. God saved the whole nation of Israel. God hears our prayer and heals our land when we humble ourselves, turn from our wrongdoing, and pray (2 Chronicles 7:14).

- Elijah prayed the prayer, "There shall be neither dew nor rain, but according to my word." Elijah walked in power and authority. He commanded rain to cease, and then the rain to come. The rain obeyed his command. God has given us authority in the earth as it is in heaven.

# WHAT DOES IT REALLY MEAN TO PRAY IN THE SPIRIT?

We don't know what to pray for, so we must depend on the Holy Spirit to pray through us. Pay close attention to the word *the Spirit* versus *the spirit*. There is a difference. In 1 Corinthians 14 when you see the word "Spirit" it is referring to the Holy Spirit or Holy Ghost. When you see "my spirit" it is referring to the spirit of man or your spirit.

We have assumed that the only way to pray in the Spirit is to pray in an unknown tongue or other tongues. However, praying in the Spirit includes praying prophetically, praying in an unknown tongue, groaning in the Spirit, revelation, word of wisdom, or word of knowledge.

Simply put, praying in the Spirit is allowing the Holy Spirit to lead and guide what you should say; how you should say it, and when you should say it. It is allowing the Holy Spirit to give you the utterance.

The utterance could be in an *unknown* tongue. An unknown tongue is a tongue that no man understands. You are speaking through your spirit directly to God. The Holy Spirit is the interpreter.

The utterance could come in *other* tongues, which is another language other than the language you are familiar with. If the only language you have learned is English and you start to speak in any other language by the Spirit of God, you are speaking in other tongues. The tongue is unknown to you because you don't know the meaning, but people who speak that language understand what you are saying.

God may use you to speak by the inspiration of the Holy Spirit in your normal language. Your normal language is considered to be a *known tongue*, which is what we call *prophesy*. Prophesy will be discussed in more detail later. Prophesy is vital in our churches today. We need a *rhema* word from the Lord. What is God saying to us? What is God saying to the church?

The utterance may come by revelation. Revelation is simply God unveiling mysteries. God loves to share secrets and mysteries of the word of God with the people of God. God wants to reveal the deep things of God to the church. However, you have to be mature to receive the meat of the word of God. God usually does not reveal the deep things unto babies because they can't handle it. Just like a baby can't handle eating T-bone steak, babies don't have teeth to chew on meat. It is too tough for their undeveloped gums to handle. Spiritual babies are similar. They don't have the spiritual stamina to be able to handle the meat of the word of God. Continue to pray that you will grow in the word of God to the point that you can handle all that God has for you and the church.

The Holy Spirit may give you utterance to speak a word of wisdom or a word of knowledge. There are times that God will speak through you concerning things from the past, present, or future. God knows exactly what is needed to bring about change and deliverance. Pray that God will give you the utterance!

A key principle to remember is that your gifts should be used to edify, build up, comfort, warn, or bring revelation. Make sure that you are being led by the Spirit of God. If you speak a prophetic word, your spiritual leader has the authority to judge your word whether it be of God or the flesh. You are accountable to the pastor of your church. If you are a guest speaker at another church, you are accountable to the pastor of that church as well. Those in ministry have to be careful not to get in pride or in the flesh and feel like they should only listen to God. Leaders also have accountability to leadership. Pastors and apostles have the responsibility to cover and look out for the people, the sheep. Wisdom is always in order. God is a God of order.

The Holy Spirit will give you what to pray; how to pray, and when to pray for a particular person, place, or thing. God already knows what was, what is, and what will be. Therefore, the Holy Spirit knows what is necessary for us to pray and when we should pray for it. Listen! Listen! Listen! Many times, we do all the talking in prayer. Make sure you take the time to listen and hear what God has to say to you and about you.

It is crucial to yield to the Holy Spirit even in prayer. You may have experienced being in prayer. Then, all of a sudden, you start praying for a specific individual or situation that was not on your mind at the time. Later, you find out the necessity of that prayer. Thank God for the Spirit of the Lord assisting us in prayer!

I remember praying concerning a situation. I had prayed in faith and stood on the word of God. Then, I began to worship and praise God for the answer. Before I knew it, I began to pray in an unknown tongue and interpret. God used me to prophesy what he was doing concerning the situation. A few minutes later, I began to laugh in the Spirit. I believe Jesus had already worked out the situation in my life, and the Holy Spirit caused me to laugh about it.

> Likewise the Spirit also helpeth our infirmities: for we know not what we should pray for as we ought: but the Spirit itself maketh intercession for us with groanings which cannot be uttered. And he that searcheth the hearts knoweth what is the mind of the Spirit, because he maketh intercession for the saints according to the will of God. And we know that all things work together for good to them that love God, to them who are the called according to his purpose.
>
> Romans 8:26–28 (kjv)

Groaning in the Spirit is a form of prayer led by the Holy Ghost. Although we may not necessarily speak in a language, the Holy Ghost still interprets even our moaning and groaning. We are yet communicating with our heavenly

Father. He knows exactly what we are saying and what we need.

Have you ever experienced praying and your heart was so heavy that you moaned and groaned? When you groan in the Spirit, the Holy Ghost is actually interceding on your behalf. God is an all-knowing God. He knows everything. We need to trust the Lord. He will give us wisdom and knowledge of what to pray for. If you want your prayers to be effectual, fervent prayers, you must be led by the Spirit of the Lord, even in prayer.

All things (situations and circumstances) will work for our benefit if we allow the Holy Spirit to intercede on our behalf by praying in the Spirit. In Acts 7:55–60, Stephen was calling upon the name of the Lord (praying in the Spirit) while being stoned to death. The Bible says Stephen was full of the Holy Ghost. Stephen saw the heavens open. He saw Jesus Christ standing on the right hand of the Father as he was being stoned. He asked the Lord Jesus to receive his spirit in verse 59. He was not moved by the persecution, because he was seeing in the Spirit.

Step out of the box and take the limits off in prayer. Continue to pray in the Spirit. Remember, praying in the Spirit includes: praying in tongues, getting revelations, prophesy, word of wisdom, or a word of knowledge. Just be led by the Spirit of God!

# PRAYING PROPHETICALLY

## PROPHESY IN PRAYER/ PRAY WITH THE UNDERSTANDING

In *Acts 10*, an Italian named Cornelius prayed. God not only granted his request, but God caused Peter to have a vision as a result of Cornelius's prayer. The purpose of the vision was to let Peter know that he needed to learn acceptance. God was preparing Peter to be able to minister not only to the Jews but also to the Gentiles. Peter went to Cornelius's house, and his whole house and other Gentiles were saved and baptized. Prayer is powerful!

Several years ago, our church was on a special consecration. I had not talked to or seen my husband since about 6:00 a.m. that morning. I was at home by myself praying. I entered into a tremendous worship. Then, the anointing to pray in tongues came. I prayed in tongues for quite some time. Suddenly, I began to prophesy over members of our local church as the Holy Spirit gave me the utterance. The last person that I began to prophesy over was my husband, who was the senior pastor of our church. As I began to prophesy and pray over him, I could actually see him kneeling down in front of a chair at church praying. It was like I was actually there. I laid hands on his head. I prophesied over his life and over the ministry. There were about five specific things that the Spirit of the Lord gave me utterance to prophesy. I wrote them down so that I would not forget.

As soon as I began to prophesy over my husband, I heard the enemy say, "You can't prophecy over a person unless they are present." Without even thinking, I said out loud, "I'm not doing this in the flesh, but I am speaking this in the Spirit!" I proceeded to speak the word of the Lord over his life until the utterance ceased.

When I finished praying, I had to leave for my appointment, which was right before our Wednesday night Bible study. As I was driving, I began to ask the Lord to give me Scripture concerning what had happened. I wanted clarity on prophesying over someone not in your presence. I had not heard any teaching on this subject or, to my knowledge, remembered reading anything in the Bible about this. I believe that anything that is of God can be confirmed through the Bible.

The Holy Spirit spoke to me while I was driving and said, "Read *1 Corinthians 14*." I thought to myself, *I have read 1 Corinthians 14 many times*. It talks about speaking in tongues, prophesy, revelation, and prayer. I still wasn't sure where this was going. I couldn't wait until I got a chance to read this chapter to get further understanding. I was waiting with great expectation to see what revelation God had for me from this chapter.

I left my appointment and went directly to Bible study. Before my husband began to teach, he said God gave him something earlier in prayer, and he felt led to share it with the congregation. He said he was on his knees praying, and there were about five specific things that the Lord gave him concerning himself and the ministry. I just sat there speechless and in awe of God's glory as he began to speak those same five specific things God gave me to prophecy over his life in prayer. It was around the same time that the Lord had given us the same thing.

God is so awesome. I believe God had actually allowed me to see him in the Spirit praying on his knees. The word of the Lord had been confirmed through both of us around the same time. Needless to say, this experience tremendously impacted my prayer life.

> Even so ye forasmuch as ye are zealous of spiritual gifts, seek that ye may excel to the edifying of the church.
>
> Wherefore let him that speaketh in an unknown tongue pray that he may interpret.
>
> For if I pray in an unknown tongue, my spirit prayeth, but my understanding is unfruitful.
>
> What is it then? I will pray with the spirit, and I will pray with the understanding also; I will sing with the spirit, and I will sing with the understanding also.

# PRAYING IN THE SPIRIT

> Else when thou shalt bless with the spirit, how shall he that occupieth the room of the unlearned say Amen at thy giving of thanks, seeing he understandeth not what thou sayest?
> 
> 1 Corinthians 14:12–16 (KJV)

Paul does a contrast and comparison of two manifestations of praying in the Holy Spirit. When you pray in the Spirit, it is the Holy Spirit giving utterance to what is needed separate from what your mind knows. The utterance can come in the form of prophesy or an unknown tongue. In the previous chapter, we discussed the difference between praying in the *spirit* versus praying in the *Spirit*. Now we will look at the difference between praying with *my spirit* and *praying with my understanding*.

God created man in three parts: spirit, soul, and body. Paul makes a distinction between praying with *the spirit*, which refers to *my spirit*, versus *praying with my understanding*. Paul is not saying, "Sometimes, I will pray with the Holy Spirit, and other times, I will pray in the flesh." What Paul is explaining is that there is a difference between praying with *my spirit* and praying with *my understanding*. He is explaining that sometimes when you pray in *the Spirit*, you are praying out of your *spirit* and using other languages unknown to you. Other times, you are praying by the Spirit out of your *understanding*, meaning your native language, which is *prophesy*. It is the Holy Spirit that gives us utterance to speak or pray in an unknown tongue as well as the utterance to prophesy.

Praying with the understanding is a Spirit-led prayer in the language that you are familiar with. You understand your prayer, because you are praying in the language known to you. You are praying a prophetic prayer.

When you pray in unknown or other tongues, you cannot understand what you are saying. Your spirit is praying by the Holy Spirit to God. You are praying in the Spirit by your spirit.

When you pray a prophetic type of prayer, the Holy Spirit is interceding on your behalf. The difference is that you understand the words that are coming out of your mouth. You just didn't know that you were going to speak those words, because it was not in your plans to say those words. The Holy Spirit uttered them through you. So you are praying in the Spirit with your understanding. You know immediately what you said, because the words were spoken in your language. With other or unknown tongues, the words would have to be interpreted, because the language is unknown to you, and you don't know what is being said.

Paul's main focus was to encourage the Corinthian church to pray in "the Spirit prophetically." He stressed that he preferred the church to make a habit of praying a prayer that is prophesy or revelation focused. When you prophesy, the whole church can be edified, because they know what you are saying. When you speak in unknown tongues, unless it is interpreted, it only benefits you (the person speaking in tongues) because no one, including you, understands what you are saying unless the Holy Spirit interprets.

Paul *does not* say, "Do not speak in tongues in church." When someone speaks in tongues and then it is interpreted, it is equal to prophesy. Just like two nickels equal a dime. You get the same results. Some people misunderstand and think you are not supposed to speak in tongues at church. Paul alludes that it is okay to speak to yourself in tongues while at church at any time. The same as you would when you pray softly. You can speak in tongues in church. Paul said he spoke in tongues more than all of the entire church. However, Paul preferred the gift of prophesy as a more effective gift to be used in the church. The gift of prophesy is more meaningful to the church, because the listeners understand the words that are coming out of your mouth.

The church at Corinth had many people that were excited about the gifts and desired to be used with the gifts. 1 Corinthians 14 provides us a guideline for using the gifts. Paul admonishes us to desire spiritual gifts, but even more so, that prophesy would be uttered regularly in the church. Prophesy will cause life to come in the church.

Prophesy will activate, stimulate, and set on fire an entire church body.

There are times when the Spirit of the Lord flows greatly in a service, and everyone is praying, worshiping, crying out to God, or speaking in tongues. No message is expected, because everyone is seeking God for themselves. However, when the leader comes to the microphone to get everyone's attention and begins to prophesy or interpret tongues, then everyone is supposed to stop and listen to what God is saying. God is a God of order! The spirit of the prophet is subject to the prophet. I don't care how anointed you think you are. You are supposed to come subject to the leadership of the house that you are in. Paul suggested that those with the gift of prophesy should prophesy one at a time so that the people could hear, and so that the word could be judged. There are some pastors that ask those that have a prophetic word for the entire church to tell them first. You are to obey the shepherd over that particular church. Your word is not going to dissipate, if it is from God, when you obey leadership. Paul was correcting the church at Corinth, because they had gotten out of order and carried away with their gifts. Everybody was excited about God using them in the gifts and wanted to prophesy and speak in tongues all at the same time. Paul was bringing structure and order to the church. God is a God of order and structure. "Let all things be done decently and in order."

Paul encourages the church to pray for interpretation. God desires that the church will flow in all of the gifts of the Spirit. We can pray to prophesy, speak in tongues, interpret tongues, and to be used in other gifts of the Spirit as needed.

I have heard ministers who have gone to various nations share how God used them to preach an entire message in other tongues. They didn't know what they were saying, but their audience understood every word, and it caused a great revival. Many were saved and delivered as a result. The key is to be led by the Spirit of God.

Remember, we are spirit, soul, and body. If you look carefully at the Spirit versus the spirit, you will better understand. When the capital *S* is used for *Spirit*, it is referring to the Holy Spirit, God's Spirit. When you see the lowercase *s*, it is referring to "your spirit."

These Scriptures also discuss that you can sing in the spirit and sing with the understanding. Prophetic singing is singing in your own native language a new song that God gives you on the spot. It is not something you heard or rehearsed before. You understand what you are saying, and yet you are singing a new song that you never heard before, because the Holy Spirit gave you the words.

You can also sing in an unknown language. When you sing in unknown tongues, you can hear the melody, but you don't know what you are saying. Yet you are still singing a new song led by the Spirit of God.

Whether you are singing in the spirit or praying in the spirit, remember at any time, you can pray for the interpretation. God can give you the interpretation of what you are saying or singing. He can also give the interpretation of what someone else is praying or singing in tongues.

Have you ever been in prayer and just started praying for a particular country, person, or specific things that your natural mind was unaware of? This is praying in the Spirit or praying a prophetic prayer. There have been times when I have prayed for a person by name, but in the natural didn't know anyone by that name. The Holy Ghost is our guide in prayer. You may not understand what the Spirit of the Lord gives you to pray, but just be obedient.

Here is another example of a prophetic prayer and a prophetic dream. Several years ago, I was praying and fell asleep. In my dream, I was praying for a young lady that I had not had communication with in over ten years. I saw her struggling and fighting with a man. It appeared that he was attacking her. It was as if I was there watching this event take place. I began to take authority over the enemy in the name of Jesus. I was interceding on her behalf. I asked the Lord to spare her life and give her another opportunity to be saved. While I was praying, I kept trying to see who the man was. It was something about the man that distracted me. I wanted to see who he was, but I could only see the young lady. I remember distinctively that the Holy Spirit said to me, "Don't concern yourself with the man, just pray for the young lady." It was so real. I woke up suddenly from my sleep, but I continued to see and pray as if I was there. I kept interceding until I felt a release in my spirit. At that point, the struggle between the man and woman was over, and I could no longer see anything. I sat there in total amazement, because I had never experienced anything like that before. This dream was so real. It was like watching a movie in my sleep.

Two weeks later, someone told me that this young lady had been attacked by her brother, but God spared her life. It was said that he was on drugs when he attacked her. This person informed me that this had taken place about two weeks before our conversation. This would have been around the time when the Lord had me to intercede for her. I also discovered why God would not allow me to see the attacker. I may have been confused about who and what to pray for.

Talk about prophetic intercession. God knows the needs of the people. I was sad in my spirit when I thought about what happened, and what could have happened. What if I had

# PRAYING IN THE SPIRIT

refused to pray for this young lady? What if I had said, "I'm too tired to pray." "I have to get up early in the morning and go to work." Prayer is vital! Many unsaved are alive today because of the prayers of their family members or other Christians. Jesus tells us that we should always pray and not faint. Don't get weary in praying for your family, friends, coworkers, and others. Keep on praying until you see your prayers come to pass.

The prayer of protection, blessings, healing, faith, and favor of God are spiritual benefits of the believers. God does rain on the just as well as the unjust. God's mercy is very great. God has given authority to the believers to bind and loose in the earth. When Jesus rose from the dead, he said that all power was given unto him in heaven and in earth. Then he told his disciples, *"I give you power."* To be a Christian means to be like Christ. We can walk in the same power and authority as Jesus. We have power with God through prayer. As you read this book, I pray that the spirit of prayer will be stirred up in you.

Jesus did not wait until there was a crisis to pray. On a daily basis, Jesus got up a great while before day and prayed. He prayed while others were sleeping. This helped to avoid others from interrupting his prayer time.

> And this is the confidence that we have in him, that, if we ask any thing according to his will, He heareth us: And if we know that He Hear us, whatsoever we ask, we know that we have the petitions that we desired of him.
>
> 1 John 5:14–15 (KJV)

We know that we have the petitions that we desire of God. When we pray in the Spirit, we know God hears us, which means he will answer by accomplishing those things in the earth.

Before Jesus told Lazarus to come forth out of the grave, Jesus prayed the prayer of thanksgiving. Then Jesus commanded Lazarus to come forth. Lazarus was raised from the dead as a result of prayer.

As a believer, it is vital to allow the Holy Spirit to lead you and guide you in prayer. You never know. Your prayer could spare a life. God would have spared an entire city for Abraham's sake, if there had been just ten righteous people. Oh! The power of prayer and the authority of the believer!

I hope that your faith is stirred up to pray in the Spirit, to prophesy in prayer, speak in tongues, worship in prayer, and sing in the spirit. Come before the Lord with thanksgiving! Worship in prayer. Pray without ceasing!

# PRAYING IN OTHER OR UNKNOWN TONGUES

*Unknown tongues* refer to a person speaking in languages that no one can understand and no one can interpret except the Holy Spirit. It is a language unknown to man.

*Other tongues* refer to a person speaking in languages that is unknown to them, but it is an actual language known to other people.

Let's take a look at how languages got started in the book of Genesis to get a better understanding of tongues.

> And they said, Go to, let us build us a city and a tower, whose top may reach unto heaven; and let us make us a name, lest we be scattered abroad upon the face of the whole earth.
>
> And the LORD came down to see the city and the tower, which the children of men builded.
>
> And the LORD said, Behold, the people is one, and they have all one language; and this they begin to

do: and now nothing will be restrained from them, which they have imagined to do.

Go to, let us go down, and there confound their language, that they may not understand one another's speech.

So the Lord scattered them abroad from thence upon the face of all the earth: and they left off to build the city.

Therefore is the name of it called Babel; because the Lord did there confound the language of all the earth: and from thence did the Lord scatter them abroad upon the face of all the earth.
Genesis 11:4–9 (KJV)

Sin had entered the earth through Adam. The people were one and had one language. God came down to see the people working together as one and making their own plans to build the tower of Babel that would reach heaven. God said, "We must confuse their language and scatter them. Nothing that they set their evil hearts to do will be refrained from them, if they work together." So God brought division amongst the people by confusing or confounding their language and scattering them. He called the name of the place Babel, which literally means confusion. Even today, you can see how people are separated by race, color, language, traditions, and values. This resulted in God confounding languages.

## PRAYING IN THE SPIRIT

And when the day of Pentecost was fully come, they were all with one accord in one place.

And suddenly there came a sound from heaven as of a rushing mighty wind, and it filled all the house where they were sitting.

And there appeared unto them cloven tongues like as of fire, and it sat upon each of them.

And they were all filled with the Holy Ghost, and began to speak with other tongues, as the Spirit gave them utterance.

And there were dwelling at Jerusalem Jews, devout men, out of every nation under heaven.

Now when this was noised abroad, the multitude came together, and were confounded, because that every man heard them speak in his own language.

And they were all amazed and marvelled, saying one to another, Behold, are not all these which speak Galilaeans?

And how hear we every man in our own tongue, wherein we were born?

Parthians, and Medes, and Elamites, and the dwellers in Mesopotamia, and in Judaea, and Cappadocia, in Pontus, and Asia,

Phrygia, and Pamphylia, in Egypt, and in the parts of Libya about Cyrene, and strangers of Rome, Jews and proselytes,

Cretes and Arabians, we do hear them speak in our tongues the wonderful works of God.

And they were all amazed, and were in doubt, saying one to another, What meaneth this?
Acts 2:1–12 (KJV)

Pentecost is a God appointed feast, which Jewish people celebrate annually fifty days after the Passover. Pentecost is first discussed in the Old Testament. It is called the Feast of Weeks. It is the feast of the open heavens. Pentecost is a time of blessings, supernatural revelation, and the fire of God being released. Isn't it interesting that God released the Holy Spirit at this time?

One hundred and twenty Christians, both men and women, were all together in one place with one accord. Suddenly, the heavens were opened. There comes a sound from heaven like the sound of a rushing mighty wind (possibly like a hurricane). It fills the whole house. Cloven (split) tongues like a fire appears, and it sits on each and every person that is present. Everyone begins to speak in other languages (tongues) as the Holy Spirit gives them the utterance.

People from every nation were present to see and hear the 120 Jewish men and women speak in their language (tongue). They had not learned their language. This confounded them. How could this be? How can a person from every nation hear someone speak in their language on the same day at the same time? The disciples were not from their country. They did not know their language.

The *Babel experience* caused the ungodly people to be confounded. They went from one language to many. This experience brought confusion amongst the people. God used this Babel experience to separate and divide the people.

Now, the reverse is taking place. During the *Pentecost experience*, the disciples had come together for a holy purpose. God used the disciples to speak by the Holy Ghost in many other languages (tongues). Everyone spoke in the language of one of the nationalities present. Many were converted and became as one in the body of Christ. Unity was brought back to the people and to the church versus division in the Babel experience.

This Pentecost experience caused a great ingathering of souls. Peter preached and explained this phenomenal experience to the nations, and 3,000 souls were added to the church that day. What a great revival! What a quantum leap! In one day the church grew from 120 people to 3,000. It started with 120 people speaking in tongues. Then, Peter preaching the Gospel of Jesus. It took one message, and one encounter with the Holy Ghost to grow the church.

This should encourage the body of Christ to know that when we, as a people, come together as one, we can do great things for God. Great revival will come when we speak the same language, the language of the Holy Spirit. One very positive thing we can learn from the Babel experience is that people can accomplish great things when they learn to work together. What would happen if every Christian focused on winning souls for Christ? What would happen if we spent hours praying and fasting? What would happen if we spent hours, days, and weeks sharing the gospel of Jesus rather than the latest gossip of the day? What would happen if we spent hours reading and hearing the word? What would happen if we practice daily being doers of the word and not hearers only? We wear bracelets that say WWJD which means, "What would Jesus do?" Do we really consider that before we act or speak? What would happen if everyone did?

We have had seasons of the holiness teaching, evangelist preaching, teachers teaching, prophets prophesying, apostles planting mega churches, pastors becoming great administrators. God has called all the ministry gifts to help mature the saints so that we would grow and be equipped to effectively take authority in the kingdom of this world and bring souls into the kingdom of God. I believe the greatest harvest and ingathering of souls is yet to come. I believe God is shifting and strategically moving Christians into place to have the greatest impact in the earth. I believe God is waiting for the people of God to return to the fear of the Lord, the passion of seeking God rather than man, and the hunger and thirst after righteousness. Then, we will see the power of God

# PRAYING IN THE SPIRIT

as not seen even in the past. I believe God is releasing a bold, wise, nontraditional attitude to the next generation of spirit-filled leaders. We will see Christians visible in powerful, decision-making positions in the earth in the days to come.

> Then they that gladly received his word were baptized: and the same day there were added unto them about three thousand souls.
>
> 43 And fear came upon every soul: and many wonders and signs were done by the apostles.
>
> Acts 2:41-43 (KJV)

Three thousand people were converted on that day of Pentecost. They continued in fellowship, breaking of bread (communion), and prayer. The Lord caused many signs and wonders to take place. The fear of the Lord was upon the church and the people. They reverenced God and his word. In the previous chapter, we discussed the difference between praying in an unknown tongue and praying with the understanding (prophesy). Remember, an unknown tongue is a tongue unknown to man.

> For if I pray in an unknown tongue, my spirit prayeth, buy my understanding is unfruitful.
>
> 1 Corinthians 14:14 (KJV)

When you pray in an unknown tongue, you are praying in a tongue *unknown* to you and to the people around you. You are speaking directly to God. Your spirit and the Holy Spirit understand what is being said. Your spirit man is edified when you pray this type of prayer. This is an excellent type of prayer to pray especially in your personal prayer time. God wants the people to be blessed, prosper, be in good health, and hear directly from him. We should maximize our personal prayer time daily by praying in the Spirit.

When we are at church, our goal should be to bless the church and the unsaved. It is the will of God for all the gifts of the Spirit to be in operation in the local church. The Holy Spirit will flow through the saints differently at various times. Sometimes, there may be utterance in other tongues, unknown tongues, or prophesy. We must yield ourselves to the Spirit of God. Our main focus, during church services, should be to edify and bless the church, the whole body, and not just ourselves. Again, Paul stressed that when we are at church that we should desire to prophesy. So begin to pray that all the gifts will be in operation in the church, including the gift of prophesy, and the gift of interpretation of tongues along with speaking in other or unknown tongues. Keep in mind that speaking in unknown tongues and then interpreting is the same as prophesy. There may be times when the Lord may cause you to pray in another language. There may be people in the church that speak fluently in the other language, and they understand what you are praying and are edified. God knows what he is doing, so just trust him.

Mature Christians seek to be a blessing, which is greater than seeking to get a blessing. Our mind-set must change. When your life becomes a blessing, blessings will overtake

# PRAYING IN THE SPIRIT

you. When you lend to the poor, you lend to God. You get what you sow. If you sow blessings, you will receive blessings. I remember one time that we were in prayer at church.

The whole church was praying. I was laid out before the Lord, and I began to speak in other tongues. I was not speaking a message to the church. I was just on my face, praying to God in tongues at the altar. The Holy Spirit gave me the interpretation of what I was praying. Later that day, my daughter asked me if I realized that I was speaking in Spanish. At the time, she was taking Spanish IV in high school. She told me what I said in tongues. It was a confirmation of what the Holy Spirit gave me through interpretation. She was amazed that I was speaking in another language by the Holy Ghost without knowing the language. This really blessed her and let her know that God is real. Praise God for the Holy Ghost! He is our guide and our leader in prayer.

A lady at my church shared that her professor said he used to be an atheist. A good friend of his talked him into going to church with her. While the service was going on, she began to speak in other tongues at her seat. He was sitting next to her and understood everything that she said. He asked her if she knew what she said, and she told him no. She was just speaking as the Spirit of the Lord gave her the utterance. He expressed to her that she was giving him a message from the Lord in a language that he had studied for years. He said it definitely made him a believer in God. He is no longer an atheist. From that day forward, he was convinced that God had to be real. He had known this young lady for a while and knew that she didn't know the language that she was speaking in. God had used other tongues as a means to draw this atheist to Christ.

An evangelist shared the testimony that when she went to a foreign country to preach, she stood up to minister, and she began to speak fluently in tongues. She spoke in tongues for over an hour. People came running to the altar. People were laid prostrate at their seats crying out to God. It was an awesome move of God in that place. When she sat down, the interpreter informed her that she didn't need him, because she had spoken fluently in their language. She informed the interpreter that she had no idea what she said in tongues. He was amazed, and the people were encouraged the more to know that God allowed her to speak their language without her even knowing the interpretation. What a great move of God as a result of speaking in other tongues.

# PRAYING FOR THE WILL OF GOD TO BE DONE

Trust in the Lord with all thine heart; and lean not unto thine own understanding.

In all thy ways acknowledge Him, and he shall direct thy paths.

Proverbs 3:5–6 (KJV)

Many times, we pray and ask God for specific things that we desire. How many people actually stop and take the time to consider if those things are the will of God? God is Alpha and Omega, which means the beginning and the end. He knows our past, present, and our future. He is the Ancient of Days. He knows us better than we know ourselves. Wouldn't it make sense to find out if the thing that we desire is the best thing for us? Just because something looks good does not mean that it will be the best thing for us. We should pray about decisions that we make concerning jobs, property, marriage, business deals, business locations, colleges, investments, church membership, etc. God is concerned about every area of our lives. He wants us to acknowledge him in all of our ways. God promises to direct our path. He will give us what to do and show us the way.

It is important for us to pray always about everything. We have decisions to make on a daily basis. We should pray for wisdom and guidance in making the right decisions. We should also pray for God ideas. One idea from God can cause you to move from having just enough to survive to having more than enough. It can also impact others. Bill Gates's idea about Microsoft changed not only his personal financial status, but it also changed the computer industry. I remember using the TRS 80 and the typewriter to type all my term papers in college. Thank God for the creative ideas that God gives to man. God is a creative God. He created man in his own image. God expects us to create, discover, explore, invent, etc.

I often think about the fact that Adam named all the animals. God watched and listened to see what and how Adam would come up with the names for the animals. God also assigned the earth to man to take care of it. God has given us brilliant minds. It is up to us to develop and use our minds, instead of destroying it with drugs and other mind altering substances.

> Then cometh Jesus with them unto a place called Gethsemane, and saith unto the disciples, Sit ye here, while I go and pray yonder.

> Watch and pray, that ye enter not into temptation: the spirit indeed is willing, but the flesh is weak.

## PRAYING IN THE SPIRIT

> He went away again the second time, and prayed, saying, O my Father, if this cup may not pass away from me, except I drink it, thy will be done.
>
> Matt 26:36–42 (KJV)

Jesus prayed at the place called Gethsemane for God's will to be done, knowing that the crucifixion was soon to take place. His mission was accomplished on the earth. Judas had conspired with the chief priest to betray Jesus for thirty pieces of silver. Jesus knew that he would be beaten and would suffer death on the cross. His purpose was to take upon himself the sins and diseases of the whole world. Jesus was about to experience a gruesome, dreadful, terrible suffering, just so that we could be saved. Jesus knew the severity of this crucifixion. Yet he still said, "Thy will be done." What great love God has for us! *John 3:16* lets us know that God gave his only begotten son. Then, Jesus, the only begotten of the Father, gave his life for us. God knew the plan and the intention of every man before the foundation of the world. Jesus fulfilled his assignment on the earth. We must also fulfill purpose even when we experience adversity.

> Likewise the Spirit also helpeth our infirmities: for we know not what we should pray for as we ought: but the Spirit itself maketh intercession for us with groanings which cannot be uttered.

27 And he that searcheth the hearts knoweth what is the mind of the Spirit, because he maketh intercession for the saints according to the will of God.

Roman 8:26–27 (KJV)

The Holy Spirit guides us in prayer. We don't always know what to pray for. The Holy Spirit makes intercession for us. The Holy Spirit can interpret our groaning and moaning. God knows our hearts and the intentions of our heart. The Holy Spirit helps us pray according to the will of God. We should continually pray that God's will be done in our lives, in the church, in our family, and in the earth.

God spoke to the prophet Samuel and told him to go to Jesse's house to anoint the next king of Israel (*1 Samuel 15:10–11, 22–23; 1 Samuel 16:1–2*). King Saul had disobeyed God more than once, and God was displeased with him (*1 Samuel 13:13, 1 Samuel 15:19–23*). God was ready to replace Saul.

When Samuel arrived at Jesse's house, he saw the oldest son, Eliab, who was tall just like Saul. Samuel thought to himself, *Surely, he is to be the next king*, but God said to Samuel, "Don't look at the height or countenance of a person" (*1 Samuel 16:6–7*). God sees the heart of man. We tend to judge people by their outward appearance. Everything that looks good is not good. That is why we should always pray for the will of God to be seen and done.

Samuel tried to pour the oil on all of Jesse's sons. The oil would not pour. Samuel asked, "Don't you have another son?" David was considered to be the least likely to be king. It was not custom for the youngest child to get the blessings or benefits of the oldest. As a matter of fact, David was not even invited to come when Samuel arrived and asked for all the sons of Jesse to come to the sacrifice. Samuel had to ask them to send for David after the oil didn't pour on any of the others. When David arrived, God told Samuel to anoint David. Samuel poured the anointing oil over David and released the anointing upon David to be the next king of Israel (*1 Samuel 16:13*). God's will is not always our will. God knew the heart of David. David loved God and served the Lord all the days of his life. He never worshipped idols. He was one of the greatest worshipers of God. David is still to this day considered to be the greatest king of Israel. He was a man after God's own heart. Therefore, God promised David that his kingdom would be an eternal kingdom. His seed would be king for generations. It is prophesied that Jesus Christ, who was a descendent of David, will one day sit upon the throne of David. It is important to find out the will of God and not make decisions based on what we see, hear, or based on the traditions of man. God's ways are higher than our ways and thoughts higher than our thoughts.

In *2 Chronicles 20*, there were three major armies coming against Judah. Judah was outnumbered. King Jehosophat didn't know what to do about the battle. So he proclaimed a fast. Families came from all the cities of Judah to join in with the king in prayer and fasting. King Jehosophat prayed, *"For we have no might against this great company that cometh against us; neither know we what to do: but our eyes are on you"*

*(2 Chronicles 20:12)*. He was looking to God for answers and direction. God spoke the answer through Jahaziel *(verse 14)*. God said that they would not have to physically fight this battle. He would do it for them. All they had to do was to praise God and watch God fight on their behalf. The singers and the praisers were saying, *"Praise the Lord; for His mercy endureth forever" (verses 21–24)*. Then God caused the armies to feel as if they were being ambushed. The armies ended up destroying each other. Who would have thought that praise would be used as a weapon to defeat an army? God's way is always the best way. He is Jehovah Nissi. The Lord is our banner. He always goes before us in battle and always causes us to win.

There are times when we have no idea what to do concerning a situation. Prayer always works! God will lead and guide you. He will instruct you what to do; how to do it; when to do it, and where to do it. We have to be patient and wait on the Lord. Waiting seems to be the hardest thing for us to do. Sometimes, we get impatient and start to say things that will lengthen our waiting time. Make up in your mind that you are going to wait patiently. Praise God while you wait. Trust God while you wait. Stay busy being productive while you wait. Continue to pray while you wait. Make sure that what you are praying and believing God for is the will of God. Never give up until you see the manifestation of the thing God has promised you!

> For ye know what commandments we gave you by the Lord Jesus.
>
> For this is the will of God, even your sanctification, that ye should abstain from fornication:
>
> That every one of you should know how to possess his vessel in sanctification and honour;
> 1 Thessalonians 4:2–4 (KJV)

We are to present our bodies holy and acceptable unto God. We have to control our own flesh from cheating, lying, killing, being envious, using drugs, taking advantage of others, etc. No one else can control our flesh but us. It is the will of God for us to treat others the way we want to be treated. It is the will of God for us to be faithful in our marriage. We cannot blame others for the decisions that we make. We can pray that God will keep us from doing evil. Even though others may do us wrong, we still have the responsibility to pray and ask God for wisdom to handle the situation. Prayer will help us to stay spiritually minded and not walk according the flesh.

Prayer involves listening to the voice of God. There are many examples in the Bible of people who chose to listen to the voice of God and learned to obey the will of God. There are a few examples below.

Noah built the ark with the specific detailed instructions that God gave him. It had never been done before. It was an unsinkable ship built by an amateur used by God. This ark housed families and every type of animal on the face of the earth. The *Titanic* was built by professionals and sunk. God's way is not always our way, but it is the best way!

God told Jonah to go to Nineveh to preach. Jonah disobeyed God and went to Tarshish. He ended up in the belly of a big fish for three days. He decided it was best to obey God. He prayed, and then the fish vomited him up on shore headed in the right direction. It pays to do it God's way! It also pays to get it right the first time to save yourself some headaches and needless trials and test.

God told Moses to lead the children of Israel out of Egypt after 400 years of slavery. Moses thought he couldn't possibly do it. He used the excuse that he had a speech impediment. Even though he did grow up in Pharaoh's house and had the best teachers and tutors growing up. God told him to take Aaron, and Aaron would speak for him. God used them to deliver millions of Israelites out of Egypt. They left Egypt with the Egyptians' silver, gold, and fine jewelry. Some of the greatest miracles took place through the obedience of Moses. God does use ordinary people. He will answer prayer. It's just not always as quick as we want. God is on a different time schedule than man.

# PRAYERS IN THE BIBLE

## MOSES PRAYS FOR GOD TO BLESS ISRAEL

And the Lord spake unto Moses, saying,

Speak unto Aaron and unto his sons, saying, On this wise ye shall **bless the** children of Israel, saying unto them,

The Lord bless thee, and keep thee:

The Lord make his face shine upon thee, and be gracious unto thee:

The Lord lift up his countenance upon thee, and give thee peace.

And they shall put my name upon the children of Israel; and I will bless them.
Numbers 6:22–27 (kjv)

You should pray this prayer often for yourself, your family, the church, and Israel. This prayer results in blessings, favor, mercy, grace, peace, and open doors.

## PRAYER OF THANKSGIVING BY DAVID

> Then went king David in, and sat before the Lord, and he said, Who am I, O Lord GOD? and what is my house, that thou hast brought me hitherto?
>
> And what can David say more unto thee? for thou, Lord GOD, knowest thy servant.
>
> Wherefore thou art great, O Lord God: for there is none like thee, neither is there any God beside thee, according to all that we have heard with our ears.
>
> And now, O Lord God, the word that thou hast spoken concerning thy servant, and concerning his house, establish it for ever, and do as thou hast said. And let thy name be magnified for ever, saying, The Lord of hosts is the God over Israel: and let the house of thy servant David be established before thee.
>
> II Samuel 7:18–26 (KJV)

This type of prayer honors God. It ministers to the Lord. We should come before the Lord with thanksgiving and praise. This prayer also was used by David as a petition for God to establish his kingdom. We should pray that God would establish our ministry, our business, and whatever we do.

## JABEZ PRAY S TO BE BLESSED AND NOT CURSED

And Jabez was more honourable than his brethren: and his mother called his name Jabez, saying, Because I bare him with sorrow.

And Jabez called on the God of Israel, saying, Oh that thou wouldest bless me indeed, and enlarge my coast, and that thine hand might be with me, and that thou wouldest keep me from evil, that it may not grieve me! And God granted him that which he requested.

1 Chronicles 4:9 (kjv)

Jabez prayed that God would bless him and enlarge his territory. He asked God to keep him from evil. Jabez realized that his name meant to bring pain, and he wanted to be a blessing and not cause harm to others. Likewise, we can ask the Lord to bless us, make us a blessing, expand our mindset, keep us from evil, and we can ask that the hand of the Lord would be upon us.

## SOLOMON PRAYS FOR GOD TO BLESS ISRAEL AND THE TEMPLE

And Solomon stood before the altar of the Lord in the presence of all the congregation of Israel, and spread forth his hands toward heaven:

And he said, Lord God of Israel, there is no God like thee, in heaven above, or on earth beneath, who keepest covenant and mercy with thy servants that walk before thee with all their heart:

And now, O God of Israel, let thy word, I pray thee, be verified, which thou spakest unto thy servant David my father.

That thine eyes may be open toward this house night and day, even toward the place of which thou hast said, My name shall be there: that thou mayest hearken unto the prayer which thy servant shall make toward this place.

I Kings 8:22–29 (kjv)

Solomon was dedicating the house of the Lord. He blessed the Lord. He asked that God would keep his promise toward David his father to bless the seed of David and continue the covenant that he made with David. Solomon wanted to make sure the name of the Lord would cover and bless this temple.

## JESUS PRAYED ALL NIGHT BEFORE CHOOSING TWELVE APOSTLES

And it came to pass in those days, that he (Jesus) went out into a mountain to pray, and continued all night in prayer to God.

And when it was day, he called unto him his disciples: and of them he chose twelve, whom also he named apostles;

Luke 6:12–13 (KJV)

Jesus prayed all night before he chose the twelve Apostles. How much more should we pray before we make major decisions in our lives?

## HEZEKIAH PRAYS FOR HEALING/ FIFTEEN YEARS ADDED TO HIS LIFE

In those days was Hezekiah sick unto death. And the prophet Isaiah the son of Amoz came to him, and said unto him, Thus saith the LORD, Set thine house in order; for thou shalt die, and not live.

Then he turned his face to the wall, and prayed unto the LORD, saying,

I beseech thee, O LORD, remember now how I have walked before thee in truth and with a perfect heart, and have done that which is good in thy sight. And Hezekiah wept sore.

Turn again, and tell Hezekiah the captain of my people, Thus saith the Lord, the God of David thy father, I have heard thy prayer, I have seen thy tears: behold, I will heal thee: on the third day thou shalt go up unto the house of the Lord.

And I will add unto thy days fifteen years; and I will deliver thee and this city out of the hand of the king of Assyria; and I will defend this city for mine own sake, and for my servant David's sake.

2 Kings 20:1–6 (kjv)

Hezekiah prayed for healing and for his life span to be extended. God added fifteen years to his life as an answer to prayer. God does hear and answer prayer. Jesus said that healing is the children's bread. Healing is a benefit of the righteous. We can claim healing for our life.

## MANASSEH REPENTED AND PRAYED FOR HEALING

And when he was in affliction, he besought the Lord his God, and humbled himself greatly before the God of his fathers,

And prayed unto him: and he was entreated of him, and heard his supplication, and brought him again to Jerusalem into his kingdom. Then Manasseh knew that the LORD he was God.

And he took away the strange gods, and the idol out of the house of the LORD, and all the altars that he had built in the mount of the house of the LORD, and in Jerusalem, and cast them out of the city.

And he repaired the altar of the LORD, and sacrificed thereon peace offerings and thank offerings, and commanded Judah to serve the LORD God of Israel.

2 Chronicles 33:12–16 (KJV)

Manasseh repented and removed the idols and altars from the house of God. He repaired the altar of the Lord and commanded all of Judah to serve the Lord God of Israel. God began to bless him. We can learn from Manasseh. When we humble ourselves, repent, and get rid of those things that dishonor God, we will begin to experience the blessing of the Lord.

## **INTERCESSORY PRAYER RELEASED PETER FROM PRISON**

Peter therefore was kept in prison: but prayer was made without ceasing of the church unto God for him.

Acts 12:5 (KJV)

And, behold, the angel of the Lord came upon him, and a light shined in the prison: and he smote Peter on the side, and raised him up, saying, Arise up quickly. And his chains fell off from his hands.

Acts 12:7

And when Peter was come to himself, he said, Now I know of a surety, that the Lord hath sent his angel, and hath delivered me out of the hand of Herod, and from all the expectation of the people of the Jews.

Acts 12:11

We should always remember that the prayers of the believers mean so much. The church prayed for Peter continuously. Peter was released from prison by the angel of the Lord. God is able to release you from bondage.

## PRAYER AND FASTING/ JESUS CAST OUT THIS KIND OF DEVIL

Lord, have mercy on my son: for he is a lunatic, and sore vexed: for ofttimes he falleth into the fire, and oft into the water.

And I brought him to thy disciples, and they could not cure him.

> Then Jesus answered and said, O faithless and perverse generation, how long shall I be with you? how long shall I suffer you? bring him hither to me.
>
> And Jesus rebuked the devil; and he departed out of him: and the child was cured from that very hour.
>
> Then came the disciples to Jesus apart, and said, Why could not we cast him out?
>
> And Jesus said unto them, Because of your unbelief: for verily I say unto you, If ye have faith as a grain of mustard seed, ye shall say unto this mountain, Remove hence to yonder place; and it shall remove; and nothing shall be impossible unto you.
>
> Howbeit this kind goeth not out but by prayer and fasting.
>
> Matt 17:15–21 (KJV)

It is crucial to remember that prayer and much fasting releases the power of God to cast out devils. This man calls his son a lunatic, because his son is suicidal. His son often throws himself in the fire, and he tries to drown himself. When Jesus cast out the devils, this man's son is made whole.

# FASTING AND PRAYER

The word *fast* has various meanings: abstinence, go hungry, swift, active, firm, loyal, devoted, nonfading, and speedy.

Fasting is considered as a time of afflicting your soul. Prayer and fasting provides great spiritual renewal, blessings, revelation, growth, direction, deliverance, and healing. There are natural benefits to fasting as well. It is said that beginning and ending a fast with eating raw vegetables and drinking steam-distilled water adds years to your life. Isaiah 58 shares the benefits of fasting and the difference between a fleshly fast and a spiritual fast.

> Wherefore have we fasted, say they, and thou seest not? wherefore have we afflicted our soul, and thou takest no knowledge? Behold, in the day of your fast ye find pleasure, and exact all your labours.

> Behold, ye fast for strife and debate, and to smite with the fist of wickedness: ye shall not fast as ye do this day, to make your voice to be heard on high.

> Is it such a fast that I have chosen? a day for a man to afflict his soul? is it to bow down his head as a

bulrush, and to spread sackcloth and ashes under him? wilt thou call this a fast, and an acceptable day to the LORD?

Isaiah 58:3–5 (KJV)

Isaiah was to cry aloud and preach against the sins of Israel and Judah. A true fast includes renouncing and turning away from sin and disobedience.

God challenges the children of God to consider their ways. As a nation, they were praying, crying out for help, expecting God to deliver them, and wanting direction, but they were still in sin and in disobedience. Their fast was a public show of piety. They were trying to look religious and spiritual to other people. They were fasting and still doing pleasurable abominable things. They were quarreling, fighting, and judging one another. Their wickedness stunk in the eyes of God. God asked the question, *"Wilt thou call this a fast, and an acceptable day to the* Lord*?"* In other words, this type of fast is ineffective and a waste of time. God is not impressed by our flesh!

God does not hear or answer our prayers when we are insistent upon doing things our way. We must repent, turn from our own way, stop sinning, and commit to doing things God's way. Until then, our fast has simply become a day that we went hungry. We can expect no results.

Now, let's take a look at a productive fast.

> Is not this the fast that I have chosen? to loose the bands of wickedness, to undo the heavy burdens, and to let the oppressed go free, and that ye break every yoke?
>
> Isaiah 58:6 (KJV)

When we truly repent, turn away from sin, and forgive everyone that has hurt us, we can expect great results from fasting. God will loose us, meaning set us free, cause a release from, disconnect, and unbind the chains of wickedness. He will rebuke the chains and cause liberty and freedom from bondage.

Many people are stuck and can't seem to get a breakthrough, because they have sworn themselves to oaths and vows that are ungodly. Some are stuck, because they allow their past to bind and hinder them from moving forward. Some refuse to let go of hurts from the past. Some people allow others to control their lives and their destiny. If you truly want to be free, you must repent and pray and ask the Lord to free you from all ungodly soul ties. Pray to be loosed and set free. Burdens can weigh you down. A burden is something that is carried. Burdens can hinder, overwhelm, cause a strain, or put a heavy load on you. Fasting will help you to lay aside the weights, sins (Hebrew 12:1), and the burdens that hinder you. God is a God that can heal the brokenhearted and the wounded spirit. He will lift the heavy burdens during the fast. We have to be willing to forgive, let go, and allow God to heal.

Oppression means to weigh heavily on or to be tormented. The term "let the oppressed go free" means to release from worry and cruel or unjust use of authority. If you have been oppressed, God will deliver you, set you free, and change your situation. He will free you from the harness that has held you down. There are many suicidal people today who are suffering from oppression and depression. Let go of the hurts and give your heart totally to Jesus. Believe that the Lord can and will set you free and you will experience a remarkable relief and immense peace.

You can experience a tremendous personal revival when you fast and pray.

> Is it not to deal thy bread to the hungry, and that thou bring the poor that are cast out to thy house? when thou seest the naked, that thou cover him; and that thou hide not thyself from thine own flesh?
>
> Isaiah 58:7 (KJV)

Many times, we get so inundated with the cares of this life, church work, careers, and family. We forget about allowing God to make us a blessing to others. Fasting reminds us that as a Christian, we are to feed the hungry, cloth the naked, and visit those in prison.

Hide not yourself from your own flesh. God already knows who we are and what we need before we even ask him. Keep it real with God! Be honest with yourself and with God. All of us have areas in our lives where we are lacking. Begin to pray, "Lord, work on me. I need to walk in love. I need to be more giving and forgiving. I am in need of patience and longsuffering. I am in need of humility and gentleness. Lord, increase my faith." God wants to bring revelation to you. When you are honest in prayer, God will reveal who you are to yourself.

> Then shall thy light break forth as the morning, and thine health shall spring forth speedily: and thy righteousness shall go before thee; the glory of the Lord shall be thy rereward.
>
> Isaiah 58:8 (KJV)

*Break* means to smash into smithereens, to interrupt, to tame as with force, to get rid of a habit, to violate a law, to disrupt the order of, to interrupt a fall, to penetrate darkness, to disclose, to decipher or solve as to break a code, to force one's way through obstacles, to stop associating with, to change suddenly, to begin suddenly (break into a song), escape, burst, crack, split, ruin, annihilate, eradicate, or terminate.

Fasting can cause your problems to be smashed into smithereens. Those old bad habits will be broken and destroyed. God will annihilate the hindrances that have kept you from moving forward. Fasting can interrupt the plans of the enemy over your life. Fasting will cause you to terminate suddenly those ungodly relationships. It will stop those unprofitable relationships that are hindering you from hearing from God.

True fasting can eradicate (uproot) hurt, pain, bitterness, jealousy, envy, pride, strife, unforgiveness, anger, rage, low self-esteem, and your past. It will cause you to be made whole.

Fasting penetrates through darkness and causes revelation to come. When your light breaks forth as the morning, you will have new revelation, wisdom, godly ideas, or witty inventions. The eyes of your understanding will be enlightened concerning spiritual matters such as salvation, the kingdom of God, etc.

Fasting will cause a sudden interruption in your physical body. Sickness will be annihilated. Speedy healing will come! Good health is a promise of fasting. Fasting will cause habits to be broken. Habits are a hindrance to our healing and recovery. Know that it is the will of God for us to be healthy and for all habits to be destroyed.

Daniel was a man of prayer and fasting. He was the best at everything he put forth his hands to do. He had all knowledge and understanding of science. He had revelation. God set him before the king. Daniel honored God, and he refused to eat the king's meat, which was worshipped to idols. He was a man that regularly fasted and prayed. He prayed three times a day to God. He didn't care who saw him pray to the God of Abraham, Isaac, and Jacob. He opened up his window and faced Jerusalem every time he prayed. He lived in a nation that knew not God. Yet he acknowledged his God and was not ashamed to serve the Lord.

Daniel's righteousness went before him when he was thrown in the den of lions, because he was caught praying to the God of Abraham, Isaac, and Jacob. God covered him by allowing him to use the hungry lions as a pillow to get a good night's sleep. God is an awesome God!

Isaiah 58:8 also says, "The glory of the Lord shall be thy rearward." The word *rearward* means rear guard or rear covering. God has your back! God will cover you from behind! Sometimes, the enemy or your flesh sneaks upon you unaware. Fasting causes the covering of God even from behind so that the enemy doesn't deceive you. If the enemy attempts to sneak upon you, God covers you and keeps you from falling. God has your back. He is a keeper! He is a covering! He is our protector! He causes us to be more than conquerors (Romans 8:37) through Jesus.

> Then shalt thou call, and the Lord shall answer; thou shalt cry, and he shall say, Here I am. If thou take away from the midst of thee the yoke, the putting forth of the finger, and speaking vanity.
>
> Isaiah 58:9 (kjv)

When we follow God's plan for fasting, all yokes, bondages, hindrances, and any other thing that holds us down will be removed by God. God will hear and answer our prayer and bring about deliverance.

> And if thou draw out thy soul to the hungry, and satisfy the afflicted soul; then shall thy light rise in obscurity, and thy darkness be as the noon day:
>
> Isaiah 58:10 (kjv)

*Obscure* means to be hidden, indecisive, unintelligible, undefined, unbelievable, mixed up, questionable, dubious, invisible, lacking clarity, confused, not easily seen, or not well-known.

If you bless others, then God will cause a spotlight to be shown on you. God will give you favor with men. Whereas, before you were hidden, you were in the wilderness, you were a no-name. God told Abraham that he would make his name great. God will give you a good name. God will define who you are. He will cause clarity of purpose to come to you. You will no longer be mixed up, confused, not knowing where you are going, or what you are to be doing. Maybe you were unintelligible, meaning unclear or not easily understood. God will reverse your situation and cause you to be understood and to understand. God will break up your dark season and cause light to come upon your life.

> And the Lord shall guide thee continually, and satisfy thy soul in drought, and make fat thy bones: and thou shalt be like a watered garden, and like a spring of water, whose waters fail not.
>
> Isaiah 58:11 (KJV)

True fasting and praying causes the Lord to guide you and prosper your ways continually. You will be like the tree planted by the rivers of water. You will have a continual overflow of abundance. You might be in the midst of a hurricane, earthquake, or any other natural disaster, but God will meet your every need and cause unexpected miracles of finances and provision. He will even make your bones fat (plentiful, healthy, profitable). You shall not want any good thing.

> And they that shall be of thee shall build the old waste places: thou shalt raise up the foundations of many generations; and thou shalt be called, The repairer of the breach, The restorer of paths to dwell in.
>
> If thou turn away thy foot from the sabbath, from doing thy pleasure on my holy day; and call the sabbath a delight, the holy of the LORD, honourable; and shalt honour him, not doing thine own ways, nor finding thine own pleasure, nor speaking thine own words:
>
> Then shalt thou delight thyself in the LORD; and I will cause thee to ride upon the high places of the earth, and feed thee with the heritage of Jacob thy father: for the mouth of the LORD hath spoken it.
>
> Isaiah 58:12–14 (KJV)

God desires us to honor him with prayer and fasting and in keeping all of his commandments. He also wants us to delight ourselves in him and in his word.

We must refrain from doing things our way and speaking what we want to speak. God expects total commitment. Then, we can receive God's promises to cause us to ride upon the high places of the earth. He will allow us to experience the best that this world has to offer. He will give us the inheritance of the blessing of Abraham, Isaac, and Jacob. We must put Christ first in our lives!

# PRAYING FOR THE NATIONS

It seems unbelievable, but there are many places in the earth that have not heard the gospel of Jesus Christ. Americans find this hard to believe, because we can turn on the television and hear the gospel preached daily. We can also find several churches to choose from in almost every neighborhood. Imagine living in a country where Bibles are not allowed, and there is no one preaching the gospel of Jesus Christ.

> But ye shall receive power, after that the Holy Ghost is come upon you: and ye shall be witnesses unto me both in Jerusalem, and in all Judaea, and in Samaria, and unto the uttermost part of the earth.
> Acts 1:8 (KJV)

We, as Christians, have become so focused on ourselves and our local church that we forget about the world. It is the will of God for us to pray for the nations of the earth and for the gospel to be preached everywhere. You may not know all the different countries or nations. Pray for the ones you do know. Invest in a map, globe, or a prayer journal that has information about the nations. Begin to read and learn about other countries, and pray that God would meet their needs.

We in the United States have never seen or experienced poverty as some of the other countries. There are places where the average income is $1,000 or less for the entire year. We consider $10,000 a year to be at the poverty level in the United States. Can you imagine making $1,000 for the whole year?

Illiteracy is high in many nations, and some have never seen a Bible or heard of Jesus. We take so much for granted. Our children have the opportunity to attend school and go to the library and learn as much as they desire to learn.

Some of us have family Bibles, personal Bibles, study Bibles, pocket-size Bibles, cassette Bibles, DVD Bibles, Bibles on our computer and smart phone. How often do we read or listen to the Bible? When we do read it, do we apply it to our lives? Let's become active doers of the word. Let us actively share the gospel of Jesus.

Pray that God would send forth laborers into the nations where the gospel has not been preached. Pray that the nations would hear the gospel preached. Pray that the eyes of their understanding will be enlightened. Pray for the leaders going to the nations that God would use them to reach the lost.

> That the God of our Lord Jesus Christ, the Father of glory, may give unto you the spirit of wisdom and revelation in the knowledge of him:
>
> The eyes of your understanding being enlightened; that ye may know what is the hope of his calling,

and what the riches of the glory of his inheritance in the saints,

Ephesians 1:17–18 (KJV)

Most importantly, pray in the Spirit concerning the nations. The Holy Spirit will give you what to pray; how to pray, and when to pray. As you are praying in other tongues, you might recognize that you are speaking Japanese, Spanish, Italian, Indian, or French, etc. It could be that you are interceding for that nation or a person in that nation. Be led by the Spirit of God. There are still many people who have never heard the gospel. You might not be able to physically go there, but your prayers are not limited.

Pray for the nations and give to those valid ministries that are spreading the gospel in the nations.

# WORDS OF EXHORTATION

## FROM THE AUTHOR

I pray that this book has given you a greater desire to spend quality time in prayer. I especially urge you to pray in the Spirit, pray for the church, spiritual leaders, governmental authorities, and the nations. It is important for us to pray and financially support the ministers and missionaries going forth to other nations to preach the gospel to the people who have never heard the gospel of Jesus Christ. Pray that God's will and purpose will be done in the earth as it is in heaven. Pray for those that have not come into the knowledge of Christ. There are many strange practices that are allowed in this nation. We need to come against witchcraft, psychic powers, rebellion, addiction, crime, abuse, carnality, selfishness, division in the body of Christ, traditions that hinder the move of God, jealousy, hatred, strife, pride, violence, terrorism and the list goes on and on.

I sincerely believe that Jesus is soon to come. We don't know the exact day or hour. We do know according to the word of God that it is soon and that we must be ready. Before that time comes, we must occupy until Jesus comes. Don't waste time on things that are meaningless! Get busy praying and doing whatever you can to further the gospel of Jesus Christ. Make the commitment right now to never let a day go by without praying in the Spirit!

Printed in the USA
CPSIA information can be obtained
at www.ICGtesting.com
LVHW021302230923
759048LV00011B/617